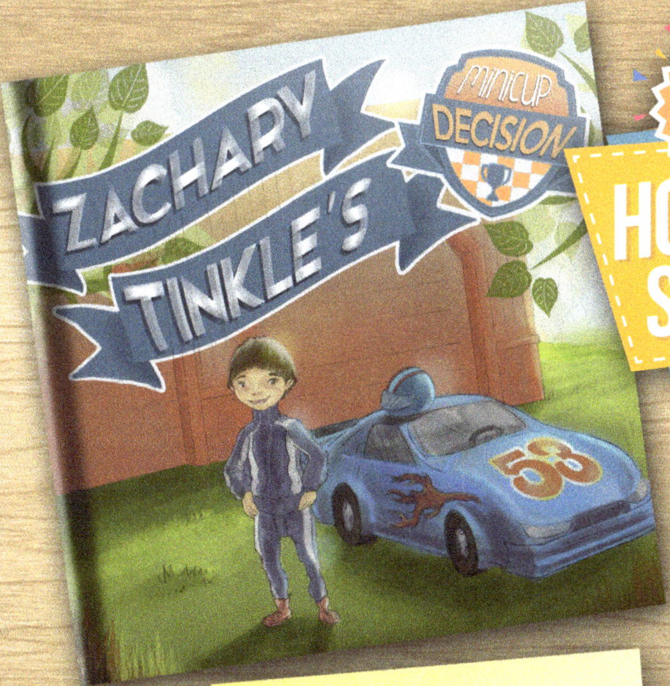

ZACHARY TINKLE'S MINICUP DECISION

#1 HOT NEW SELLER

A story of making tough decisions and the courage to passionately pursue your dreams!

A book on the uphill battle of competition when you're the underdog that inspires kids of all ages to never give up!

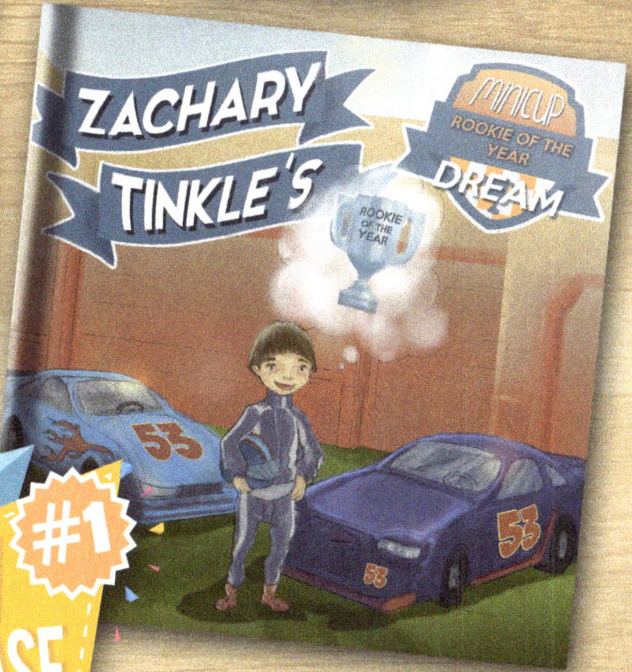

ZACHARY TINKLE'S MINICUP ROOKIE OF THE YEAR DREAM

#1 NEW RELEASE

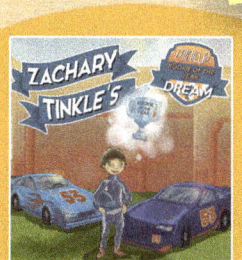

TAMBIÉN EN ESPAÑOL

www.LeftPawPress.com

Plumb pug craziness and pet fashion obsession combine to teach about pet rescue and the unbreakable bonds between humans and pets

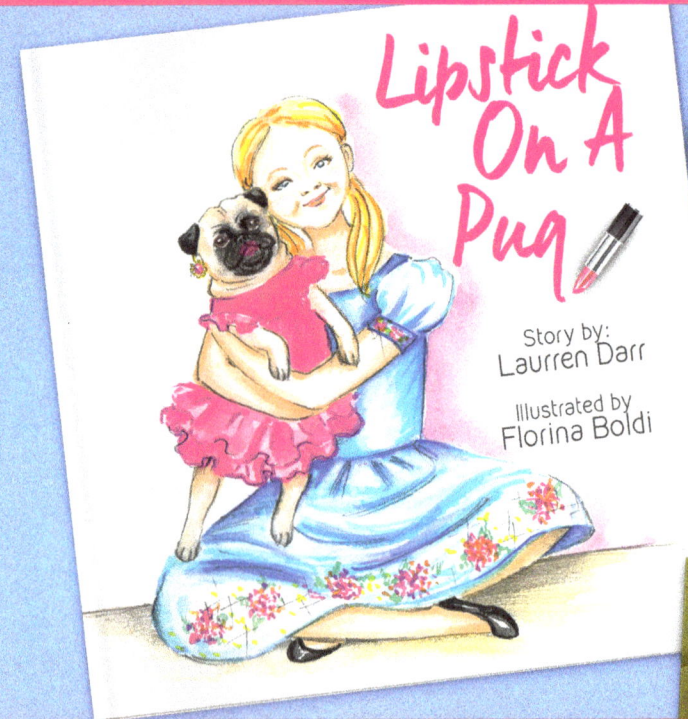

CHILDREN'S BOOK OF THE YEAR 2015

Timid rescue pug turns into an outgoing dog with a belly rub fixation

Text and illustrations copyright © 2019 Laurren Darr /Left Paw Press

All rights reserved. No part of this book may be reproduced or transmitted in any form or by any means, electronic or mechanical, including photocopying, recording, or by an information storage retrieval system, without express written permission from the publisher.

Left Paw Press, publishing imprint of Lauren Originals, Inc.

Contact us on our publisher's website at:
www.LeftPawPress.com

ISBN: 978-1-943356-67-6

Library of Congress Control Number: 2019901985

PRINTED IN THE UNITED STATES OF AMERICA

Author: Laurren Darr

Illustrations: Antonio J. "Nunoh" Díaz

It all started years ago. My favorite boy and race car driver, Zachary Tinkle, had started racing a half scale stock car called a minicup. My family was going to have photos taken. They wanted pictures with me and Zachary with his race car and they wanted us to match.

The next thing I know, the photo of me sitting in my replica car was featured in *Speedway Illustrated*. They called me the 'Pit Pet Fashionista.' I was featured in *Dogster* too!

Then, I had cameo appearances in a couple children's books about Zachary's decision to start stock car racing and his winning rookie of the year.

It was pretty cool hearing about all the great things Zachary was doing at the race track.

Suddenly, something changed. My pet sitter had a family emergency one weekend and couldn't watch me while the family needed to go away for Zachary's race.

Mom found a pet-friendly hotel and I got to go to the race track and be in the pits!

After the races, the track opened the gates and let fans come into the pits. It was so fun meeting all those people. I lost track of the belly rubs and back scratches I got. If I may say so, I was quite an attraction.

While they were petting me, people would ask some of the same questions about the minicup cars. I can hear the answers in my head, "It's a half scale stock car with the features of full size cars so it's a good learning race car. It has an engine capped at 20 horsepower that will go up to around 70 miles per hour when Zachary is running in the top five."

Kids were allowed to get in Zachary's race car and take photos. They loved that.

The most important thing was that I got to be with my family. Zachary made sure he came and hung out with me. There were times when I could tell he just needed to get away from people and something might be wrong. There were the other moments too. I was there for the wins when Zachary would get shiny trophies. You should have seen him jump with joy when he won the Illinois State Championship at Grundy County Speedway.

When he won the National Short Track Championship, he got a massive trophy from Rockford Speedway.

One of the best nights was when he did a clean sweep at Anderson Speedway. That means he was the fastest qualifier and won both his heat and feature races. He handled his on-track interview like a pro.

Before we knew it, there was talk about Zachary 'moving up' and we spent a lot more time at the tracks that year with his team so he could practice in the full size car. It was a big jump. He had to learn to shift a manual transmission.

The horsepower went up to 425 in his McGunegill Engine Performance motor. He practiced over 2500 laps in the late model while competing for the minicup series championship. It seemed like, if we weren't AT a race track, we were traveling TO or FROM one.

By then, we had more photos taken and they got me another car to look like the full size car called a late model that Zachary was training in. Mom had a tutu made by Doggie Diva Boutique. It matched the colors of Zachary's suit with his number 53 and name on the back. She also had a shiny collar made with the number 53 in a bedazzling red.

That year, they even made a set of hero cards with me on them!
That's the year Zachary won the minicup series championship.

The next year, Zachary raced full-time in the full sized late model car. He was with a team and I didn't get to go to the track as much, but loved every minute when I did. I do wish I could have been there at Winchester Speedway when he won his first late model heat race.

I heard my family talking about how cool it was that fellow teams gave Zachary a standing ovation when he drove back into the pits.

I would have had my tail wagging and paws in the air too! He went on to win Sportsman of the Year and Most Popular Driver, even though he was rookie. (I'm pawsitive it's because of my support and voting).

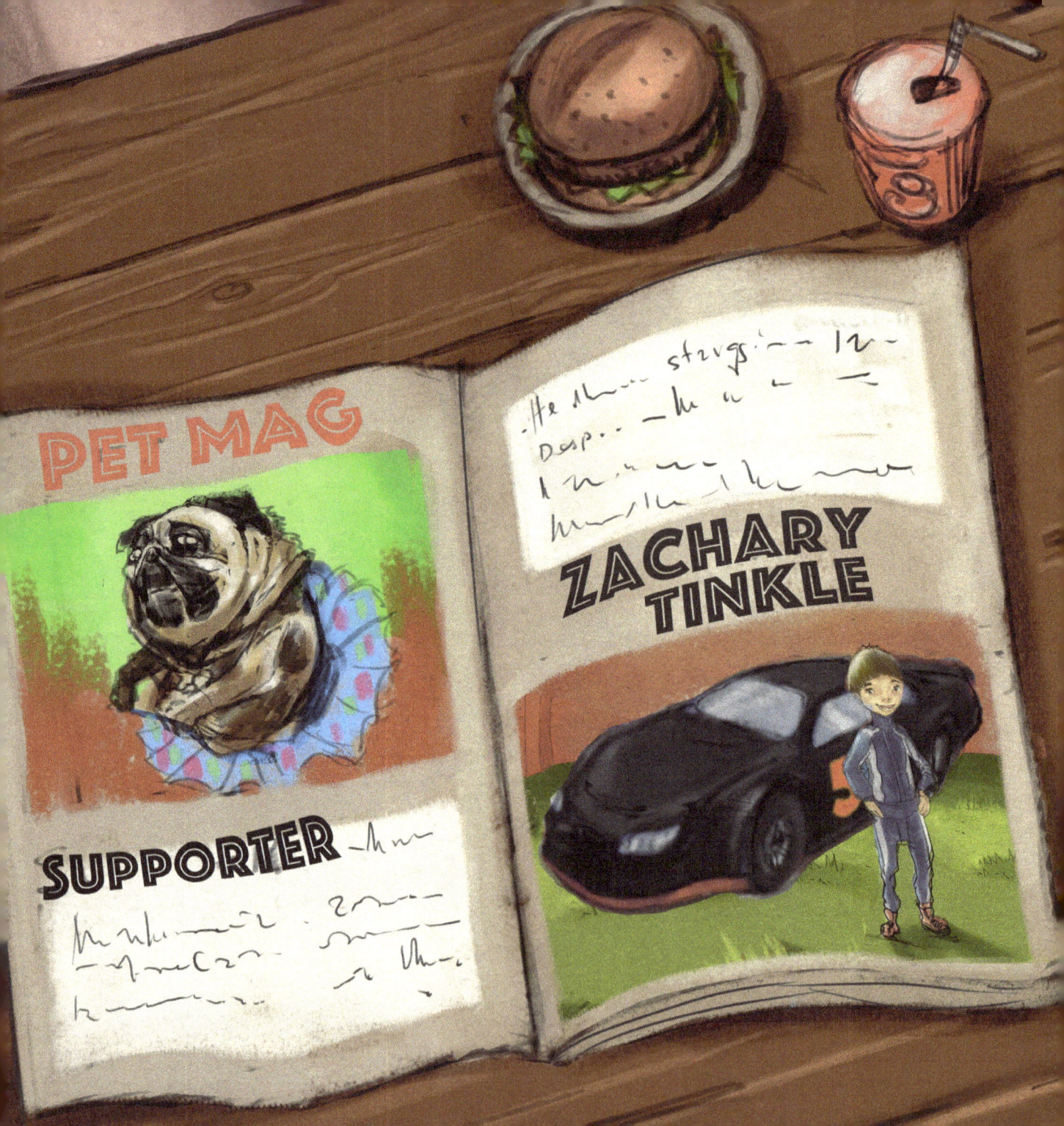

Even though I wasn't always there, word of my being his most loyal supporter continued to spread. Zachary and I were featured in both *AKC Family Dog* and *Boomer Pet Magazine*.

I'm not sure where things will go from here, but I hear the family talking about Zachary racing another year in the Vore's Welding CRA late model sportsman series and at Anderson Speedway in the McGunegill Engine Performance late model series with our own team. AND, they're having a new race car built by VanDoorn Racing Development. I hope I get a new car that looks like his and a new tutu to match his new Hinchman race suit so I can still be the most stylish dog in the pits. Paws crossed I get to go to some races, meet fans, and get even more belly rubs!

RELIEVE STRESS BY *Coloring*

Keep checking LeftPawPress.com for even more pet-related mandala coloring books.

About The Author

Laurren Darr has been 'owned' by pugs since her first pug rescue of White Pines Tuttie when she was just six years old. Tuttie had never been out of a cage or even uttered a bark. She was the joy of Laurren's life until she left this world at the age of 15 (human years, of course!). This silly pug would let Laurren dress her, put clippy earrings on her, and even put lipstick on her. They'd spend hours tootling around the neighborhood dressed in their Sunday best, which is why Tuttie served as the inspiration for the launch of the Pet Fashion Guild over thirty years later.

She understands the deep roots and connections created between humans and animals through fashion because of this kinship. Her book, "Lipstick On A Pug," won the Dog Writers Association Maxwell Medallion for 2015 Children's Book of the Year. Her publishing imprint, Left Paw Press, has printed numerous books on pet fashion, pug children's, medical, racing, and coloring. "PugDala Coloring Book," a mindfulness coloring book, also won a Maxwell.

In 2013, Laurren combined her marketing experience and lifelong love of pet fashionology to launch the Pet Fashion Guild, an organization created to provide educational materials and tools for pet fashion professionals. She's been named a "Paw-er Woman" by Fidose of Reality blog and was a 2015 & 16 finalist for Pet Industry Woman of the Year. In 2018, Pet Age named her a Woman of Influence. Laurren earned her pet fashion certification from Fashion Institute of Technology (FIT) in New York City in 2015.

Laurren's busy Indianapolis-area home is filled with her husband, her race car driving son (Zachary Tinkle), and a fabulously fashionable pug named Bella.

BOOST YOUR PET BIZ MARKETING!

Get the ultimate trade show conference 'in a box' with timeless interviews conducted for the Unleashable summit. You'll gain amazing marketing and industry insights from several different high profile people in the pet industry. Interviews include the following:

- Pet Industry Attorney
- Pet Industry Publisher
- Pet Industry PR Person & FIT Professor
- Pet Industry Trade Show Executive
- Pet Industry Editor-in-Chief
- Pet Industry Video Producer
- Pet Model Stylist
- Pet Blogger
- Pet Industry Financial Executive

Find out more information at www.PetFashionGuild.com

Cat & Dog Breeds
FASHION FITTING GUIDE
Laurren Darr

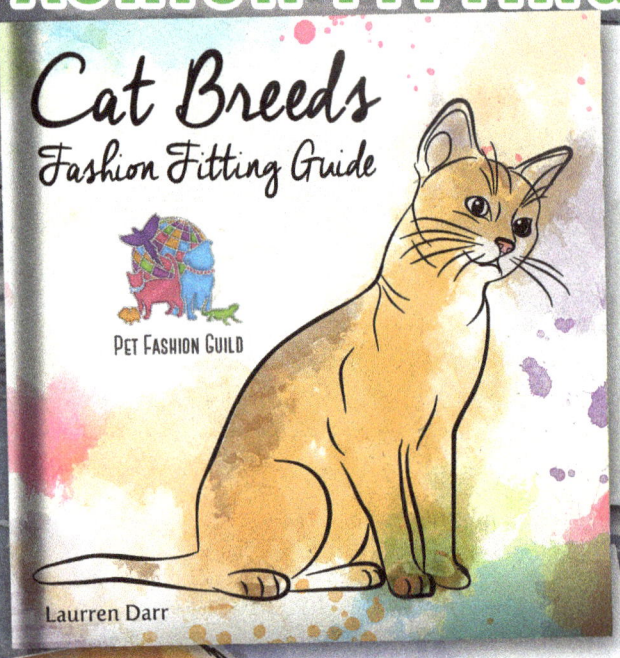

www.PetFashionGuild.com

www.LeftPawPress.com

www.PetFashionGuild.com

Get the most comprehensive dog fashion illustrations set along with design considerations in the Dog Breeds Pet Fashion Illustration Encyclopedia book set. Includes all of the AKC breeds separated by the seven breed groups.

Companion Coloring Books
ALSO AVAILABLE

www.PetFashionGuild.com

MEDICAL BOOKS BY
DR. BRAD T TINKLE

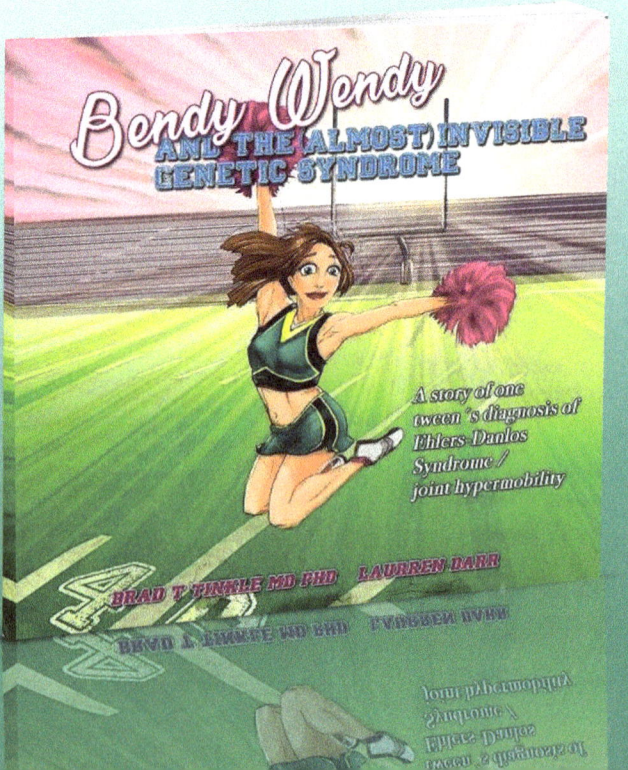

www.LeftPawPress.com

www.ingramcontent.com/pod-product-compliance
Lightning Source LLC
Chambersburg PA
CBHW060948170426
43201CB00023B/2419